# The ultimate business skills collection from Bloomsbury Business

The new *Business Essentials* series from Bloomsbury Business offers handy pocket guides on a wide range of business topics – from writing a CV and performing well in interviews, to making the most impactful presentations, finding the right work/life balance, brushing up your business writing skills, managing projects effectively, and becoming more assertive at work.

**Writing Skills for Business**
How to communicate clearly to get your message across

**Manage Projects Successfully**
How to make things happen on time and on budget

**Assert Yourself**
How to find your voice and make your mark

**Succeed as a New Manager**
How to inspire your team and be a great boss

**Balance your Life and Work**
How to get the best from your life and still have a life

**Give Great Presentations**
How to speak confidently and make your point

**Get that Job: Interviews**
How to keep your head and land your ideal job

**Deal With Stress**
Improving your health through changing how you work

**Get that Job: CVs and Resumes**
How to make sure you stand out from the crowd

Available from all
as well as

BLOOMS

# Give Great Presentations

*How to speak confidently and make your point*

BLOOMSBURY BUSINESS

LONDON · OXFORD · NEW YORK · NEW DELHI · SYDNEY

BLOOMSBURY BUSINESS
Bloomsbury Publishing Plc
50 Bedford Square, London, WC1B 3DP, UK
29 Earlsfort Terrace, Dublin 2, Ireland

BLOOMSBURY, BLOOMSBURY BUSINESS and the Diana logo are trademarks
of Bloomsbury Publishing Plc

First published in Great Britain in 2005 by Bloomsbury Publishing Plc
Revised edition published in 2010 by Bloomsbury Publishing Plc
(under the A&C Black imprint)
This revised and updated edition published in 2022 by Bloomsbury
Publishing Plc

A catalogue record for this book is available from the British Library

Library of Congress Cataloguing-in-Publication data has been applied for

ISBN: 978-1-4729-9325-0; eBook: 978-1-4729-9326-7

2 4 6 8 10 9 7 5 3 1

Text design by seagulls.net

Typeset by Deanta Global Publishing Services, Chennai, India
Printed and bound in Great Britain by CPI Group (UK) Ltd, Croydon CR0 4YY

To find out more about our authors and books visit www.bloomsbury.com
and sign up for our newsletters

# Contents

# Assess yourself: How good are your presentation skills?

If you're reading this as a presentation is looming, take heart! This book will help you conquer your nerves, get your message across and give a great performance. Start here by answering these questions and reading the guidance points.

**How do you feel about public speaking, either in-person or online?**

a. I hate it.
b. I prepare very carefully to avoid nerves.
c. I always enjoy it and never get too stressed.

**How do you deal with nerves?**

a. I don't really. I just have to get on with it.
b. I try to take it in my stride. I think being a bit nervous helps me to perform.
c. Although I do get nervous, I always pretend that I don't and bluster my way through by playing a role.

**Do you practise?**

a. Yes. I often try to improve my presentation at the last minute.

b. I rehearse four or five times but when I feel I have got it right, I don't tinker with it.

c. I don't bother to rehearse. I know I'll be fine.

## How long do you usually make your presentations?

a. I keep it as short as possible.

b. As long as it takes to cover all the necessary ground.

c. As long as it takes – I really enjoy public speaking.

## How do you deliver an in-person presentation?

a. I often fiddle with my hair or props as I get so nervous.

b. I stand up straight and make sure I address my audience directly throughout the presentation.

c. I tend to sit down and relax.

## How do you deliver an online presentation?

a. I turn off my camera so that no one can see me.

b. I make sure I talk into the camera, not at the screen.

c. I've never really thought about it; it's just a chat, right?

## Do you cater your presentation to your audience?

a. No, not really – I just want to get my point across.

b. Yes. I try to find out as much about them as I can beforehand.

c. Yes. I tend to aim it at the most senior people.

## How long do you arrive before you are due to give an in-person presentation?

a. I'm always a few hours early.

b. I like to leave enough time to check my equipment.

c. I'm often late.

## What would you do if everything went wrong?

a.  If I'm honest, I'd completely panic.
b.  I'd keep smiling and try to keep calm.
c.  I don't think I'd be too bothered. I'm not likely to see the audience again.

a = 1, b = 2, c = 3

Now add up your scores.

**9–14:** The very thought of presenting makes you nervous, so take some action to calm your nerves. Chapter 6 will help with this particularly, but Chapters 1, 2 and 3 feature lots of practical tips on planning and research that will help make your life easier, too. They'll help you work out your objectives, so that you know exactly what message you want to get across. Read Chapter 8 and find out how you can and will survive if things don't quite go to plan!

**15–20:** Well done – you've realized that practising is the key to a great presentation! Chapter 7 will show you how you can take your performance up a notch further still by boosting what you say with the way you say it. Chapters 4 and 5 offer lots of advice on how you can boost your message with the clever use of visuals and images; Chapter 3 talks about the specifics of online presentations

**21–27:** It's great that you enjoy presenting; it's a really useful skill to have and will stand you in good stead as you move up the career ladder. Try not to be over-confident, though, and take the time to tailor what you say to your audience – you'll really grab their attention then. Chapters 1, 2 and 3 are particularly helpful here.

# 1
# Preparing great presentations

Giving a presentation, whether in-person or online, can strike fear into the heart of even the most experienced business people. It takes some courage to deliver a well-structured and interesting talk to an expectant audience, and most of us at one time or another have experienced the panic, sweaty palms, blank minds and wobbling voices that sometimes accompany this.

Being able to cope with presentations is a very valuable skill, though, whatever your job. They are useful in many situations, such as pitching for business, putting a case for funding, addressing staff meetings or even as part of the application procedure for a new job. Few people like speaking formally to an audience, but there are many real benefits and, as you gain experience in giving presentations, you'll probably find that it becomes less of a worry, and even enjoyable.

This chapter offers you help on the first step of your journey towards a great presentation: preparation. It will give you some suggestions for preparing the content of what you're going to say, looking at your objectives, gearing it to your audience and getting your points across well.

## Step one:
## Work out your objectives

Clear objectives are the starting point for all great presentations. Start by working out your objectives – ask yourself why you're giving the talk and what you want your audience to get out of it. Think about whether using speech alone is the best way of communicating your message or if your message might benefit if you were to use visual aids and slides to further illustrate its main points.

When you're planning and giving the presentation, keep these objectives in mind at all times – they'll focus your thoughts. Having an objective for giving the presentation will ensure that you're not wasting anyone's time, either your audience's or your own.

For example, let's say that you're presenting a new product to your company's sales reps at your annual sales conference. Your objectives in this case may be to:

- introduce your product to them positively and enthusiastically;

- talk them through the benefits of your product;

- point out the many advantages it has over any competition;

- explain why the target audience would want to buy it.

**TOP TIP**

It's very important that you believe in what you're going to be talking about. This is particularly the case if you have to deliver a difficult message, such as one related to change or something that others are likely to perceive as bad news. These situations are bound to be uncomfortable and if you don't wholeheartedly believe in your message, others will be able to pick this up. It won't necessarily be as a result of anything you say, though; your body language may give it away without you even noticing. See Chapter 7 for more information on this.

**Step two:**
**Find out what you need to know about your audience**

Before you plan your presentation, try as best you can to find out who is going to be in your audience and their expectations. For example, the tone and content of a presentation to the managing director of another firm will be very different to one addressed to potential users of a product, or to one directed at people you know well. It's important that you know the extent of the audience's knowledge about the topic you'll be discussing, as their familiarity with the subject will determine the level at which you pitch the talk and the language you use (see below).

✓ Whatever the interests of your audience, try to appeal to what will motivate and interest these people. For example, if you're talking to senior people in your company about a new product, you might want to include information about how it can be produced cost-effectively; if you're talking about a new way of doing things, stress how much more effective it will make your team. If you're talking to reps who'll be selling the product for you, you need to highlight how much better it is than the competition. As you can see from these examples, you need to 'tune in' as far as you can to your audience's needs. A few hours doing the groundwork will be time very well spent.

### Step three:
### Make sure you've got your facts straight

Once you know why you're speaking and who you're talking to, you can firm up your ideas about what you're going to say.

Get back to basics by checking that you have all the main facts straight. For example, if you're talking about a product or service, make sure you know:

- its current name (remember that this may have changed many times!);
- its price;
- when it will be ready;
- what it's meant to do;
- how it works, if appropriate;
- benefits;
- what the competition is.

If you're talking about a new process, find out about:

- why you're changing from an existing way of doing things;

- what the changes are;

- when they'll take effect;

- what benefits they'll bring.

> **TOP TIP**
>
> If you're giving your presentation just after you've come back from holiday or a business trip, take a few moments to check a few key facts with colleagues before you speak. Some key elements of your presentation (such as prices, names, delivery dates) may have changed while you've been away and the last thing you need is to have someone pipe up from the back to correct you. It will boost your confidence to know that you're on top of things!

## Step four:
## Begin writing your speech

When it comes to presentations, there's no substitute for detailed preparation and planning. While everyone prepares in different ways, all of which develop with experience, there are a few key points to bear in mind while you're preparing.

✓ Start by breaking up the task of preparing your speech into manageable units. Once you know the length of the presentation – let's say 15 minutes – break up the time into smaller units and allocate sections of your speech to each unit. For example, you might want to give two minutes to a general introduction, six minutes to a discussion of your main theme, two minutes to sum up key points and five minutes to take questions. All of this will depend very much on your topic and audience, however, so don't try to shoehorn your presentation into a very rigid format – keep things fluid if you need to.

✓ Note down all the points you want to make and order them logically. This will help you develop the framework and emphasis of the presentation.

✓ Keep your presentation short and simple if you possibly can, as it will be easier for you to manage and remember.

A shorter presentation is usually more effective from the audience's point of view, too, as most people dislike long presentations and will not necessarily remember any more from them.

---

**TOP TIP**

If you need to provide more detail as part of an in-person presentation, you can either:

1. Supply a printed handout to your audience at the beginning. Try to do this only if the information is essential to understanding the talk; otherwise you'll be fighting to make yourself heard over the rustling of paper!

2. Share your slides, via email, after the event.

✓ Avoid overloading your talk with facts and figures; a few well-placed numbers can help illustrate a point, but it can be hard to maintain an audience's interest if they are being bombarded with figures. Instead, use some graphs or charts to illustrate what you're saying. Aim to identify two or three key points and think about ways you can get these across creatively.

✓ Don't use too much jargon. It may be tempting, especially if you work in a technical industry, but bear your audience in mind at all times – if you've followed the steps above and done some research on them, you'll know how familiar they are with your theme, and not everyone will be a specialist. If you do need to use abbreviations or acronyms, explain early on what they mean so that everyone can follow you. You can always recap in your handout, if you provide one, or list them on your website.

## Step five:
## Visual aids and equipment

Both online and in-person presentations often benefit from the use of visual aids, such as PowerPoint. However, although slides have become ubiquitous, don't make them do the work: remember that visual aids should only be used as signposts during the presentation, to help the audience focus on the main point you're trying to make.

✔ If you do decide to use them, try not to cram too much information on to one slide or screen, as you'll lose your audience's attention while they try to read everything on it. Make sure the audience can see the information by using big, bold, simple lettering, and bear in mind that images are often far more effective than words.

Turn to Chapter 5 for step-by-step advice on this topic.

**Step six:**
**Practise!**

OK, so you know what you want to say, who you're aiming it at, and your slides are ready. It's time to put everything together and practise.

✔ Practise as much as you need to make sure that you're very familiar with your speech – allow plenty of time for rehearsal before the event. This is important for both in-person and online presentations. Even if the presentation has been sprung on you with very little notice, run yourself through it at least three or four times. Reading your text out loud, timing yourself and making sure that the slides and your speech run at the same speed are all great ways to be sure that your presentation will run smoothly. Don't panic if your mind goes blank when you start off; keep calm, go back to the beginning and start again. There may be points where you feel that you'll never get it right, but you will and you'll find a rhythm that carries you along.

**TOP TIP**

Once you're confident that your presentation is right, don't tinker with it! You may have heard it many times, but your audience won't have. Changing things at the last minute is just giving you more stress that you don't need.

✓ Also practise using the equipment you intend to use; we've all experienced the horror of not knowing how to turn on a projector in front of a room full of people or experiencing a wi-fi outage in the middle of a pitch. If you're in-person, check you know how all of the venue's equipment works and how to synch it up with your computer or phone. If you're running an online presentation, test everything (e.g. laptop, microphone, camera, sound), check that you know how to share slides/ your presentation in the chosen software (not all video conferencing packages are the same) and turn off all notifications from emails and social media to avoid your audience being interrupted by pings. If you're presenting from home, you might want to find the most wi-fi-friendly spot for your computer and ensure that everyone knows not to interrupt you.

✓ Have a contingency plan to cope with any unforeseen mishaps. For example, whether in-person or online, print out your slides/speech so, if something goes wrong with them you have the presentation details to hand and can carry on speaking.

See Chapter 8 for more help on what to do if things don't go to plan.

**TOP TIP**

If you're going to run the presentation from someone else's site, it's a good idea to email the file to yourself or store it in a cloud-based provider so that you can access it wherever you're giving the presentation. This means that you can always access the file on someone else's computer if your own stops working.

✔ Time your speech during rehearsals to make sure that it is taking the time you'd estimated. You'll probably also need to allow time at the end for a question-and-answer session. Try not to rely on your notes in the presentation, because it can be overwhelming trying to find a salient detail from a file or sheaf of paper; instead list the main points on numbered index cards, to provide reminders. Whether online or in-person, these will help you maintain eye contact and not lose your flow.

**TOP TIP**

Using cards rather than a printout has lots of advantages. You can move through the cards much more easily than you can do with several pages and you can also add notes to yourself to help you speak more confidently. This can be anything from 'breathe!' to 'emphasis here' to 'pause here' – whatever works best for you.

## Step seven:
## Think about the venue

✓ If you're giving your presentation at your company's office, book or arrange an appropriately sized room as soon as you know you're going to have to speak. Make sure there's enough seating for your audience and that lighting, ventilation and heating are all working properly.

### TOP TIP

Ask a colleague to stand at the back of the room in which you're going to speak so that you can make sure you're speaking loudly enough. If the room is very big (a boardroom in a large organization, say) or even a small one with poor acoustics, it might be worth finding or asking the company to invest in a proper microphone. They're inexpensive and can be used time and again.

✓ Organize some refreshments for participants, such as tea, coffee and water. You also need to make sure there will be no interruptions, for example fire drills or people accidentally entering the room. Put a sign up on the door that states the time the meeting is due to begin and how long it will go on for. If your talk has a title, such as 'Motivating your sales team' or 'New products for ABC Ltd', you could add that, too.

**TOP TIP**

If your company has a reception, it's a good idea to let the staff know that there'll be an influx of guests on the day. Guests can then be pointed in the right direction and they can let you know when they start to arrive so that you can be ready to greet them.

✔ Wherever you present, from home, at your company's office, at another location, you must make sure that any equipment or props you need are available and set up properly before the presentation starts. If you're presenting at a conference or a client's premises it's a good idea to visit the site beforehand to make sure it has everything you're expecting. It's even a good idea to check out where the switches or plug points are, so that you don't get caught out on the day.

**Common mistakes**

✗ You don't find out about your audience

A good knowledge of the audience is absolutely crucial in finding the correct pitch. It's no good blinding your audience with technical jargon if they only have a basic grasp of the subject. Similarly, a very knowledgeable audience will soon switch off if you spend the first few minutes going over the basics.

✗ You talk for too long

If your presentation absolutely has to be longer than 20 minutes, insert some breaks so that your audience remains fresh and interested and you can have a sip of water to keep you going.

✗ Not checking the room and equipment for in-person presentations

This can be disastrous! Imagine, for example, arriving and finding that there's no facility for delivering PowerPoint presentations and you have no other method of showing slides. Make sure you're familiar with the environment in which you'll be presenting.

## BUSINESS ESSENTIALS

✓ Make sure you have clear objectives for your presentation. Know what you want to say and why.

✓ Believe in what you're saying; if you're unsure of or unhappy about your message, the audience will pick up on it.

✓ Find out about your audience. This will help you 'pitch' the presentation well.

✓ Make sure you're up to speed about all the basic facts relevant to your presentation, such as prices, deadlines, specifications, benefits, competition and so on.

✓ Prepare, plan and practise thoroughly.

# 2
# Delivering great in-person presentations

A presentation is an ideal environment for you to promote your ideas, your products or your services. You have a captive audience, you can provide them with relevant information and are there on the spot to answer any questions they may have. For a presentation to be a success you must be able to hold the attention of the audience and leave them wanting to know more.

Some people are natural presenters, while others find it more difficult. If you fall into this latter group, don't worry; practice and feedback from previous audiences will help you develop all the necessary skills. In Chapter 1, we found out about how to get ready for the presentation; this chapter will help you deliver it with confidence and style.

**Step one:**
**Look at the structure of your presentation**

Structure is essential for any presentation. There should be an introduction, a main body and a conclusion. You can be witty, controversial or even outrageous if the mood of the presentation allows, but whatever approach you try, your chief aim is to arouse the audience's curiosity and to get your message across.

### Introduce your presentation

The introduction to your presentation needs to attract your audience's interest and attention.

A good opening will also boost your own confidence, because if you start well, the rest should follow easily. Plan your opening words carefully for maximum impact: they should be short, sharp and to the point.

- If appropriate (that is, if you're speaking externally at a conference or internally to people you've never met before, such as prospective customers or suppliers), introduce yourself briefly. There's no need to go into too much detail; just tell them your name, job title and the broad subject you're talking about.

- Let your audience know how long your presentation will take, as this will prepare them to focus for the period of time you expect to speak.

- Summarize the contents of your presentation, so that your audience can work out how much information they'll need to absorb.

- Explain how the presentation will work in terms of the audience's interaction with you; tell them if you'll be taking questions at the end or if you're happy for them to pipe up as you go along.

**TOP TIP**

Explaining the key points in the first few sentences will also help your mind to focus on the task in hand and refresh your memory on the major points of your presentation. It sometimes helps to get started if you can learn your first few sentences by heart.

### *Make an impact in the main section of the presentation*

It goes without saying that the main section of your presentation will be driven by the key points you want to make.

✔ For maximum impact, use short, sharp and simple language that will keep your audience's attention and also make sure that your message is being understood.

**TOP TIP**

✔ Include only one idea per sentence and pause after each one, so that you make a mental 'full stop'.

✔ While you do need to be precise in what you say, make sure you don't sound too stilted or as if you're reading something out of a book – it's good to give the impression of spontaneity.

✔ However nervous you feel, stick to your original plan for your presentation and don't go off at a tangent on a particular point and miss the thread. Why not try using metaphors and images to illustrate points? This will give impact to what you say and help your audience to remember what you've said.

### *Conclude your presentation*

Close by summing up the key points of what you've covered. The closing seconds of your presentation can be as crucial as the opening sentence as they give you an opportunity to really hammer home your point. To make the most of this, think about what action you'd like your audience to take after the presentation is over and then inspire them to do it.

For example, let's say you've been presenting your new star product to your company's most loyal customers. You want them to love the product as much as you do, to buy it in large numbers and to sell it with gusto. Remember that this is where your enthusiasm for, and belief in, your message can truly make a difference, so:

- be brief, but speak clearly without rushing;

- quickly restate the product's advantages or benefits;

- emphasize your hopes for the product (for example, you believe it will be the market leader in X months' time);

- if it's an option, offer them an incentive, such as if they buy early, an X% discount or a multi-buy offer.

### Step two:
### Think about your posture and delivery

Now that you know what you'll be saying, it's time to think about how you can say it best and definitely make a splash.

✔ Maintain eye contact and address your audience directly throughout your presentation.

✔ Be aware of your stance, posture and gestures without being too self-conscious. Don't slouch, as you'll look unprofessional. Standing up straight will make you appear more confident and will also help you to project your voice better.

### TOP TIP

Always stand, rather than sit, when you're doing a presentation. Don't fiddle, for example with a pencil or your phone; try to keep still and avoid moving around excessively. All these things are distracting for an audience and will mean that they may miss some of the important points you're trying to get across.

✔ Remember that your audience has come to learn something. Try to sound authoritative, sincere and enthusiastic. If you don't sound as if you believe in yourself, this will come across to the audience.

✔ Think about the way in which you're speaking. Most people need to articulate their words more clearly when addressing an audience. There's usually no opportunity for the audience to ask you to repeat a word they've missed, so aim to sound the vowels and consonants of words clearly.

✔ Think about the expression in your voice, too. Try to vary the volume, pitch and speed of delivery to underline your meaning and to keep up your audience's interest.

**TOP TIP**

Think about your facial expressions, too. Obviously, if you're talking about a contentious issue or have to tell a group of people bad news, you're not going to be all-singing, all-dancing as you take the podium. But if your presentation is a more general one, or is sales-orientated, it's good to smile! Smiling at your audience will give the impression that you're at ease and that you're looking forward to talking to them.

## Step three:
## Answer any questions

Some people prefer to take questions at the end of a presentation rather than have their flow of concentration interrupted while they're speaking. This is a good strategy if you're nervous or if you're talking about a complicated or very technical subject – it's all too easy to lose your way.

✓ If you do take questions at the end of a talk, give your audience an idea of how much time you have to spend on it; this may be an issue if you're just one of a number of people speaking in a particular session, as if you run over, everyone will start running late.

✓ If someone asks you a question and you don't know the answer, be honest and tell the other person that you'll find out what they need to know and get back to them separately. This will save time and also prevent you from giving an incorrect answer.

✔ Encourage interesting discussions between members of the audience by throwing general discussion points open to the floor once you've said your piece (or even if you haven't!). This tactic may be appropriate if you're speaking to an audience made up of your peers or of specialists in a certain subject; you may all learn something from it.

## Step four:
## Make a dignified exit

Once the question-and-answer session is over, you're just about done. All that remains is for you to say thank you to the audience for listening. If you have material to circulate, now is the time to do it. It's a good idea to include your contact details/social media handles on these handouts so that people can get in touch with you about questions that occur to them later, or hopefully to indicate some interest in what you've been talking about. Thank them for their feedback and keep in touch if you can; giving presentations is a great way to network and build up your contact list.

### TOP TIP

Watch where you're going! If you've been nervous about doing your presentation, you're bound to be heartily relieved that it's all over. In your eagerness to take your seat elsewhere, don't rush off stage in case there are tricky steps to negotiate. Also keep an eye out for cables, leads, plugs or even chairs in the way – you don't want to bump into them and ruin the great impression you've made.

## Common mistakes

✗ You're not enthusiastic

If you're not interested in what you have to say, don't expect your audience to be. Listening to a single voice for 20 minutes or more can be difficult for an audience, so you have to inject some enthusiasm into what you're saying if you are to keep them with you (and awake!). To help keep things going, activities or discussion with your audience, as mentioned above, can help a great deal.

✗ You speak too quickly

Don't rush your presentation; it's important to take your time. It's hard not to go quickly, especially when you're nervous and want the whole thing over with as soon as possible, but the audience will find it difficult to understand you or to keep up, if you talk too fast.

Make sure you summarize your main points every five minutes or so, or as you reach the end of a section. This will help to pick out the most important issues for your audience, and it's then more likely that they'll remember the central issues long after you've finished your presentation. As discussed in Chapter 1, practising with a colleague or friend will help a lot here, as they can tell you how you're doing in terms of the speed of your delivery.

✗ You don't check the equipment

There's nothing more irritating for an audience who have all made an effort to turn up on time than to have to sit around and wait while you struggle to get your laptop to work or sort your slides out. Make sure everything is exactly in place well before your audience begins to arrive.

✗ You don't interact with the audience

Be careful not to look at the floor during your presentation or to direct your speech at one person. Try to draw your whole audience into the presentation by glancing at everyone's faces, in a relaxed and unhurried way, as you make your points. Keeping in tune with your audience in this way will also help you judge if people are becoming bored. If you do detect that people are glazing over, you could try to change the tempo of your presentation to refocus their attention.

✗ You're late!

We all have days when absolutely everything seems to go wrong, but as far you can, try to make turning up late to your own presentation the last thing you need to worry about. Leave yourself twice as much time for your journey as you think you'll need. This will allow for getting lost several times en route. If you're driving or taking the train, check your local news before you leave to see if there are any hold-ups. If the presentation is more than a few hours' drive away and you're on quite early, see if your company will foot the bill for you staying overnight nearby.

**BUSINESS ESSENTIALS**

✔ Be sure the structure of your presentation works.

✔ Pay attention to your posture and delivery.

✔ Be ready to answer questions.

✔ Thank your audience.

# 3
# Delivering great online presentations

Online or virtual presentations are different in some ways from those given in-person. However, their purpose is the same – to convey information in a concise way that makes a real impact. And, given the impact of the COVID-19 pandemic on working practices, they are an essential way of communicating with colleagues, clients and business partners.

The pandemic aside, there are many reasons why people choose, or must, present virtually or online. Whatever the reason, your presentation must still reinforce the image, brand and overall message of your company, engage the audience's attention and answer as many of their potential questions as possible.

The first two chapters' explanation of how to prepare and how to deliver in-person presentations has lots of relevant information for an online presentation. In addition, there are other specific details that will need your attention.

## Step one:
## Make sure the tech is working

1. Check your laptop/computer is charged, that your broadband is functioning and that your mobile phone (if not being used) is switched to silent. Also check that you have logged into the right video-conferencing account: there's nothing worse than being full-flow on a great Zoom presentation when you see a pop-up telling you that you are nearly at the limit of your 40-minute free time slot.

2. Learn how to use the software: if you are presenting on different or new video-conferencing software, take some time before the session to learn how it works. You will then feel more relaxed both when starting and managing the session. Learn how to mute your audience, how to let an audience member share if necessary and how the chat or polls work so that you can make full use of them. Mastering the interactivity is key to animating the presentation and engaging with your audience.

3. Preparing your slides: be sure that your slides are readable on your own computer screen, so that they will be readable on others'. Also, check that you know how to upload them to the video-conferencing software you are using as well as how to share, open, read, move and close them while, at the same time, speaking to your audience.

## Step two:
## Lighting and set-up

1. If you are presenting online from a professionally lit venue or office, it is likely that the lighting for your

presentation will be perfectly suitable. However, if you are presenting online from home, it is worth thinking about the set-up. Ideally, you will be presenting in the daytime, facing a window, with plenty of natural light falling on to your face. If this isn't possible, try different set-ups, using desk lamps, light boxes or ring lamps as required, then record and watch yourself back until you are satisfied that you appear as naturally lit as possible, and not in shadow or blindingly bright.

2. Background: set yourself up with a relatively neutral background behind you. If this is not possible, try one of the blurring background tools offered by video-conferencing software but be aware that this can be equally distracting, because it can blur you if you move about while presenting.

## Step three:
## Make the most of your camera

1. Look at your camera, not your screen

   Professional television presenters are well trained at looking at the right spot in a camera, rather than the camera operator, but, for the rest of us, it requires practice. Learn where your web-cam is and train yourself to look at it, rather than at the faces on your screen. If you find this difficult at first, try rehearsing with your mobile phone: look at the camera on your phone, record yourself looking at it and then watch it back. At first, you will find your gaze drifting away and this will be obvious when you watch yourself. However, gradually you will become more accustomed to looking at the camera dot, not at a friendly face.

2. Ask your audience to turn their cameras on; it is much nicer to talk to people's faces than to a black screen.

3. If your own image is a distraction, turn the self-view off if this is available. This way, you can look at your audience, not in a mirror.

## Step four:
## Don't forget to set yourself up!

1. Clothes: don't think that, because you are behind a screen, you don't need to pay attention to what you wear. First, the better dressed you are, the more confident and professional you feel, and this will come across in what you say. Second, if your audience sees you presenting in a scrappy T-shirt or your pyjamas, they are less likely to take you seriously and respect what you have to say. Be comfortable, but smart.

2. Smile: just like clothes, what we are feeling is visible in the way we talk. So remember to smile and relax; no one enjoys watching a miserable, frazzled presenter.

3. Keep their attention: during the COVID-19 pandemic, many people tired of watching the world from behind a screen. Mastering the interactivity of your software is key to animating the presentation and engaging with your audience. Use the chat, and polls as needed, to break up your talk.

## Step five:
## Manage the format

As with an in-person presentation, make the parameters of the session explicit from the outset: tell them how long it will be, what the format is, whether there will be time for questions and how much. Then stick to that plan because, as soon as you run over time, your audience will begin to switch off. No one likes a presentation that over-runs; everyone loves those that come in short! Also remember to take plenty of breaks.

## Step 6:
## Manage interruptions

If you are presenting from work, this should be relatively straightforward. Shut your office door or book a room where you can have some privacy. Switch off all phones (unless you are using your mobile). Turn off all email notifications that may ping on your computer set-up. At home, make sure you inform the whole household that you need peace and quiet, find a space in a room where you can close a door if possible and put pets (and children!) in other rooms to be looked after by someone else (the cat can go out...). Finally, make sure that no one is streaming videos or downloading large files at the same time as your presentation (this will reduce your broadband speed and the functionality of presenting over the Internet) and unplug the doorbell.

When planning your own online presentations, think about those that you have been part of. What did you like about them? What did you hate? Make a list of good techniques and bad, then try to copy the good ones and avoid the bad!

## BUSINESS ESSENTIALS

✓ Ensure your tech set-up works.

✓ Check your lighting and background.

✓ Use your web-cam to your best advantage.

✓ Dress and behave professionally.

✓ Stick to your presentation structure and format.

✓ Prevent or minimize interruptions.

# 4
# Creating on-demand presentations

Sometimes it is not possible, or desirable, to present live. Perhaps the time difference doesn't work, perhaps you need to share the information to several different people or clients, or perhaps it is more time- and cost-effective to create a shareable, repeatable presentation. But, just as with live presentations, you still need to consider how your presentation looks and 'feels', how you can involve the people reading it and what technology or software you use to create it. The guidelines below will help set you on the right path.

## Step one:
## Think about the length and format of your presentation

Again, as with a live presentation, the first and most important things to decide are who your audience will be, exactly what you want to say to them and how to deliver this information. You might choose to be filmed giving the presentation as if you are in the room with your audience, with or without slides; you might choose to narrate a deck of slides, without showing your face; or you might employ another company to produce the presentation for you. The possibilities for the latter are endless so we will be focusing on the presentations you produce yourself.

There is one big difference between live and on-demand presentations: since you won't be there to further explain the slides, visuals or screens, each will have to contain all the explanation necessary. In other words, instead of simply being the written back-up to your speech, this presentation must stand alone. As a result, it will be very tempting to either talk for too long or write yards and yards of text to explain everything properly. Don't go there!

### TOP TIP

To get the amount of copy/speech roughly right, write out your presentation text as if you were going to deliver it to an audience in-person. Then cut it in half. Then cut it in half again. That way you will be left with the important essence of what you want to say and none of the extra 'fluff'.

### Step two:
### Get the look and feel right

As with other kinds of presentation, it is important that the look and feel of an on-demand presentation are consistent with the rest of your company image, so that your audience receives the same key messages from it as they would from any other contact with your business (see Chapter 5 for more information on this). In fact, it's even more important in this case as, once again, you won't be there live to reinforce the impression it creates.

In addition to this, there are other considerations when designing the look of an on-demand presentation.

If you are producing a presentation that will involve a lot of reading, it is important to remember that reading on screen is much harder on the eyes than reading on paper, so:

- avoid cramped text and use as much white space as possible;

- use a light background with dark text;

- be careful in your choice of colours. Although these should complement your corporate colours and logo, bright tints like reds and yellows can be dazzling on a screen and difficult to read; paler shades or dark colours are easier on the eyes;

- choose a simple, non-serif font (like Arial) and a standard font size of 10–12pt;

- illustrate and enhance key points with tables or simple graphics;

- aim to keep each page to one screen in length, as most people prefer not to have to scroll too much.

**TOP TIP**

Web page designers work on the premise that reading speeds are more than 25 per cent slower on computer screens than on paper. But that doesn't mean you should write 25 per cent less – you should write 50 per cent less.

How you structure your text is also important, as people rarely read screen pages word by word; instead they scan the page, picking out individual words and sentences. To cater for this, your copy needs to be very clear and easily readable in order to get the message across quickly.

Here's a list of pointers:

- keep your sentences short and punchy;

- make sure that each line is no more than about 12–13 words long;

- highlight important keywords so that they catch the reader's eye;

- use one idea per paragraph and keep paragraphs short – no more than three to four lines each;

- break up the text wherever appropriate with sub-heads, bullet points and numbering;

- make sure your spelling and grammar is top-notch. Many people adopt a friendlier or more casual tone in virtual communications than might apply to other business materials, but spelling mistakes and grammatical howlers are a step too far.

### TOP TIP

Inconsistency or poor-quality design will detract from your image and may even lose you business. Attention to detail, on the other hand, will automatically ensure you come across as professional and even compensate for small shortcomings in content.

## Step three:
## Think about adding some 'drama'

A big advantage of online presentations is that you can use all sorts of effects to make your information more dramatic and interesting, and thereby catch your audience's attention.

While the important rule here is not to overdo it – less really is more! – here are some ideas:

| Effect | Description |
|---|---|
| Orchestrating of information | Use of a pointer to guide the viewer: this could be an ordinary screen pointer or an animated character of some kind. Try not be too cutesy with this type of thing, though – it might be a good idea to use a character if it ties in with your company logo, for example, but don't go overboard with cuddly toys. |
| Reveals | This technique allows one piece of information at a time to be presented to the audience, frequently by using a 'grey-out' facility that hides content and reveals it in gradual stages. |
| Build-ups | Similar to the reveal, this technique allows information to be added in stages. |
| Overlays | This usually involves the complete image being presented, but each 'overlay' then highlights or expands on the initial image. It can be used to highlight paths through complicated diagrams. |
| Variety | While all your slides should have a uniting look and feel, it could become boring for the viewer if every screen looks identical. Make sure that there's some variety between them, such as colour-coding different subjects. |

## Step four:
## Be user-friendly

When you're creating your presentation, it's important to keep the needs of your audience in mind. They are probably busy people with limited time, so you need to make it as easy as possible for them to understand and access the information you're providing.

✓ Explain clearly what your presentation is about as soon as you start or on the first slide. There's nothing more annoying for people – or anything more likely to lose attention – than trying to work out what you are talking about. Think perhaps about beginning with a summary of the information you are presenting and, if you are just using slides, include links that click directly through to different sections so viewers can go straight to areas of interest.

✓ As with a good website, a slide presentation should be easy to navigate. Try to give readers more than one way to access the information – for example, by having navigation buttons down one side as well as links at the bottom of each page, and cross-reference hyperlinks within the text. If there's a lot of material to get through in your presentation, you might even want to include a simple search facility.

✓ If your presentation requires a lot of detailed information – such as technical specifications, for instance – think about putting it in separate appendices rather than in the main body of the slides. That way, anyone who needs the in-depth information can find it, while at the same time your main deck remains uncluttered.

✔ Make it easy for readers to contact you should they have questions or require further information. Make sure your company's email address, phone number and social media details can be read clearly and are prominent.

## Making on-demand video presentations yourself

If you're self-employed or working from home, you may have to make on-demand video presentations without access to an in-house tech team, using your phone and a tripod. As anyone who has a social media account will know, self-made videos are often an essential part of both personal and business brand strategy, and are also used more and more by universities, schools and government departments. However, there are so many different options, and ways to make them, and the area is changing so rapidly, that it is beyond the scope of this book to offer more than an outline of how to proceed.

### Be honest

First, before you spend any time or money on making a video, ask yourself if it is realistic and a good use of your time to make it yourself? Also ask yourself if your phone and a tripod will provide the quality you need for your purposes or whether you will need to upgrade it or borrow/rent a camera?

If it is going to take you five days, and those five days cost you £1500 of work time, is it going to be cheaper and more cost-effective to employ a professional to do it in a day? Are you being honest about your skills, the time it will take and the quality you can create? Be sure to consider this first.

## Research a platform that suits you

Investigate all the various platforms and apps that are available and/or ask someone you know who has experience of them for advice on which ones are the best. They all offer templates and instructions to help you get started. However, not all of them will be suitable for making videos at home or on a phone so try some out before committing/paying for a professional version.

## Research what you want your video to be and do

Depending on what and who you are making the video for, you need to be clear about what it could or should do. Consider this a free-for-all for a few hours spent watching Instagram, YouTube and TikTok! Go and look at your competitors and other companies you admire, to see what sort of video output they use, to see what is possible, engaging and memorable and think about the following while doing so:

- What and who it is for?

- How long should it be?

- Do you need props?

- Can it be filmed at home or do you need another setting?

- Do you need music or animation?

- Do you need any other people or voices in it?

## Make some test videos

This is not a Zoom with your friends; this is a professional presentation so it needs to be as good as it can be. Once you have decided on your platform and started planning what you want, start making some dummies. For a start, you will quickly learn both what it is possible to do, with your time and resources, and what is out of reach. If possible, share these with colleagues or friends and ask for feedback.

## Do your prep

As with live presentations, both in-person and online, you still need to follow the tips outlined in the rest of the book:

- know your audience;

- prepare well: e.g. make notes or cards, or create another form of prompt so that you are not reading when presenting;

- present yourself professionally;

- have a contingency plan ready for any problems. Obviously, for an on-demand video, you can edit out issues later; however it is good to think about what might go wrong and how to fix it, to save yourself endless retakes.

**How to present yourself**

As with live presentations, both in-person and online, you still need to follow the tips outlined in the rest of the book:

- know your audience;

- prepare well;

- present yourself professionally;

- have a contingency plan ready for any problems.

## Step five:
## Think about common queries in advance

Try to anticipate likely questions that people might have after watching or reading your presentation. Providing the answers in a separate section – perhaps in the form of frequently asked questions – will show you're ready to help and may encourage them to contact you. And it may also save you time and money by nipping some basic queries in the bud, such as requests for your opening hours or prices of the products you're promoting.

## Step six:
## Involve your audience

One disadvantage of not presenting your information in-person is that it is much harder to make your audience feel involved. However, there are various techniques you can use to hold their attention.

✔ Interactivity

Interactivity is one of the greatest strengths of online presentations and it's a good idea to make yours as active as possible. Consider if you can offer online tools such as calculators or quizzes viewers can fill in. These help them feel involved and – if they're useful – will also encourage them to return to your presentation.

### ✔ Changing content

If your presentation is featured on your website somewhere, you can extend its shelf life considerably by adding visibly new content on a regular basis. Perhaps you could offer a new tip each day or provide a weekly news service to give visitors a reason to return. This is known as 'sticky content'. Remember, to do this you will need to be able to access the presentation to make changes; it will also take a certain amount of time and effort on your part.

### ✔ Freebies

People are more likely to remember your presentation, and return to it, if they got something useful or free out of their last visit. Is there something you can include that will add value? Offering something, such as a discount or a preview of a new range or sale prices, in exchange for an email address, is also a great way to build a mailing list.

BUSINESS ESSENTIALS

### TOP TIP

It is essential that your material is up to date – readers will be put off immediately if there's something obviously obsolete on your presentation, such as an old date at the foot of it. If the material needs to last some time, consider removing anything time-sensitive from it and keeping dates as vague as possible, perhaps restricting them simply to the year of publication.

## Common mistakes

✗ You get carried away

There are so many exciting tools, effects, gadgets and gizmos that it can be very easy to make your presentation far too busy. Always remember that less is often more and that the main point of your presentation is the information you are trying to convey, not your artistic skills or technical wizardry.

✗ You don't make your presentation easy to access

One vital thing that's easy to forget is how your audience is going to access this presentation of yours. If it's too complicated or cumbersome, involves esoteric technology that readers don't possess and need to download, you will lose them straight away.

As ever, the answer lies mainly in knowing your audience, but generally speaking, it's best to keep things as simple as possible. If in any doubt, get expert advice – either from your IT department or from someone experienced in such matters. It would be a pity to fall at the last fence and waste all your hard work!

## BUSINESS ESSENTIALS

✓ Keep your text short, snappy and punchy.

✓ Check that the look and feel matches the rest of your corporate image, and that it works when displayed on screen.

✓ Add some drama – though judge it carefully.

✓ Be sure that your presentation is user-friendly and easy to navigate.

✓ Try to anticipate and answer likely queries arising from your material.

✓ Use clever techniques to involve your audience.

✓ Don't get too carried away with snazzy or unnecessary details and effects.

✓ Make sure that your presentation is not too complicated or high-tech to be easily accessible.

# 5
# Using slides and visuals in your presentations

It's a very common mistake – particularly for those who are new to presenting – to feel that it's necessary to produce a huge number of slides, containing all the information being discussed, as well as all sorts of complicated and sophisticated diagrams and visuals. You'll be relieved to know that, thankfully, this isn't the case!

In fact, the golden rule is: all written or visual material is only there to back up and give emphasis to what the presenter is saying. That's it. If the audience requires further material or detailed information, it is far better to produce this as handouts, if in-person, or as an appendix/link to a website if on-demand. Otherwise, the watchwords are simplicity and clarity.

This chapter provides a series of rules and suggestions which, if followed, will help you to create a presentation that has all the impact necessary, but may also save you considerable time and effort.

## Step one:
## Think about 'brand consistency'

Whether you're creating slides, visuals or any other kind of presentation material, it's important to make sure that your audience receives the same key messages from it as they would from any other contact with your business. In other words, the presentation needs to portray the same brand as your website, stationery, sales and marketing materials, offices, signage or any other promotional literature you might have. If it is not consistent, it may well have a negative impact on how your audience perceives your image in general, so it's worth spending the time to get it right.

Think about the following factors when designing the overall look of your presentation:

- a specific typeface;

- your logo and letterhead design;

- a particular colour or palette of colours;

- any text that needs to be included on every slide – perhaps your website address or business slogan, for example.

**TOP TIP**

Even if you're not representing a company or organization, you still need to create a consistent, professional 'brand' for your presentation. Choosing or designing a particular template as the basis for each slide or overhead is a great place to start and will save you time in the long run.

If you're using PowerPoint, use the 'Slide Master' page to design your overall look right at the start. By setting up your fonts, sizes and colour scheme here, and inserting any logo you want, they'll appear on every slide and you won't have to format each one individually.

## Step two:
## Create text slides

When creating text slides for in-person presentations, there are four main rules to bear in mind. Get these right and you're well on the way to having an effective presentation.

### 1 *Make it BIG*

You need to choose a font size that's big enough for everyone to read – even from the back row. As a rough rule of thumb:

- for text in bullet points use a font that's at least 24pt in size;

- for any added detail, use text of at least 18pt.

## 2 *Keep it simple*

Most people tend to put too many words on a slide, and it's important to get rid of all unnecessary text. You don't want your audience's attention to be fixed on trying to read a long slide rather than listening to you. The guidelines are:

- no more than six lines of text per slide;
- no more than seven words per line of text;
- use colour to attract attention to important points – for example, keywords could be highlighted in a different shade.

## 3 *Make it clear*

Choose a clear, non-serif font (like Arial) and write in upper and lower case – text that's all in capitals is difficult to read. You also need colours that enhance the readability of your slides. Most of PowerPoint's default font sizes and colour schemes work well; if you decide to experiment with your own, be sure that you don't reduce readability in the process.

> **TOP TIP**
>
> If in doubt, dark colours on a light background tend to be the easiest to read.

## 4 *Follow a logical sequence*

In order to clarify your message for your audience, the stages of your presentation and the slides you use need to follow a logical sequence. Here are a couple of useful ideas:

✓ Begin and end the presentation with an identical pair of slides, which summarize your main points. At the beginning, this gives the audience a notion of what to expect and helps you conquer last-minute nerves by reminding you of what you want to say. At the end, it provides a way to recap your arguments and also gives the audience the sense that you've come full circle, completing the 'story' you promised them at the beginning.

✓ Create 'signpost' slides, or slides that remind the audience at intervals where you've got to in the presentation and how each part fits into the whole. This is a very good way of keeping people's attention – particularly if the presentation is a long one.

> ### TOP TIP
>
> Your audience must be able to get the point of a slide within five seconds of seeing it. When you put up a new slide, don't say anything for a few moments – let people absorb the information. Then, when you have their undivided attention, expand upon what the slide has to say.

### Step three:
### Decide on the right visuals

A picture is worth a thousand words, they say – and it's certainly true that a verbal message that is reinforced with a visual one is stronger than the verbal message alone. So visual aids, which in this case means any sort of illustration, graphic, graph or diagram that you might want to use, are certainly an important part of most presentations.

However, there's a problem: while a good visual gives a huge boost to a presentation, a poor one leaves it worse off than no visual at all. At best, it distracts the audience; at worst, it baffles them. So if you're going to use visuals, it's essential that you use them well.

Your first question, then, when planning your presentation shouldn't be 'What visuals do I need?', but 'Do I need any visuals at all?'. Here are three benchmarks to help you decide whether a visual is necessary or not:

1.  Does it back up your argument? Any visual that doesn't reinforce what you're saying will simply distract the audience.

2.  Does it clarify a tricky point? Using a picture is sometimes the only effective way to explain something complicated, for example how a machine works or how different statistics compare with one another.

3.  Does it make an impact? If there is just one important message you want your audience to take away from your presentation, can it be summed up in a single image?

**Step four:
Design your visuals**

*Use pictures, not words*

The best question to ask yourself when designing a visual is, 'What does this show?' (rather than 'What does this say?'). In other words, use as little text

as possible. If you do need to add words – labels
on graphs, titles on organization charts, stages on
workflow diagrams, for example – make sure:

- they're still in a decent font size (18pt minimum,
  preferably);

- they're horizontal wherever possible, for ease of
  reading;

- even if they have to be vertical (along the
  axis of a graph, for instance), the letters are
  horizontal.

### Try some icebreakers

Sometimes it can be helpful to use a visual early on
as an icebreaker that will warm up the audience and
get you over the jitters. Presenters often make this
a 'funny', which is fine, but you do need to be a bit
careful: if you're not a natural joke-teller, it can be
embarrassing all round if your story falls flat. Cartoons
can also do the job for you, but again, make sure the
content and implications of the cartoon suit the rest of
the presentation.

### Titles for visuals

Too often, presenters make the mistake of putting a
general label, such as 'Sales in last quarter' at the top
of a visual. However, it's much better to come up with
a very specific label that tells people what you want
them to look at in that visual. Instead, if you wrote
'Sales in last quarter reverse previous downward trend',
your audience would know instantly why they're being
shown this slide. The key message here is: make the
title of a visual the same as its message.

## *Choose the right kind of chart*

Charts are the ideal way to convey information instantly. However, different charts are appropriate for different kinds of information. Here's a quick checklist:

| Purpose | Chart type and description |
|---|---|
| Showing change over time (e.g. share prices) | Line charts. The slope of the line instantly tells viewers the direction of the trend. |
| Direct comparisons over time (e.g. how operating costs have risen faster than manufacturing costs over three years) | Vertical bar chart. The height of the bars shows the comparative costs; and because people naturally associate left-to-right with the movement of time, vertical bars work better than horizontal ones where there's a time element involved. |
| Direct comparisons at one time (e.g. the building society with the lowest interest rate in March) | Horizontal bar chart. The length of the bar gives its ranking; the label on it identifies the item. |
| Comparing parts of a whole (e.g. the percentage of government budget spent on education) | Pie chart. This is the simplest way to show proportions, as long as there aren't too many slices (five maximum is ideal). |
| Comparison by geographic location (e.g. sales by region) | Map. Distinguish among regions by using different colours, shadings or symbols. |

## *Build up an image*

If you have a complicated concept to communicate, it can be very effective to break your image up into stages and introduce them one at a time. PowerPoint is the ideal medium for doing this.

Say, for example, you're showing an intricate organizational design. You could start with the top executives, then add the directors who report to them, then the group managers, then the departmental heads and so on. You could do this in a number of ways:

- sequentially – separate diagrams for each part, which you show one at a time;

- build-ups – where each new layer is added individually, one on top of the next;

- reveals – where you start with the whole diagram, but most of it is covered up to begin with and sections are exposed gradually.

Remember that you may not need to include every single detail of the new organization in the diagram; just make sure it contains the bits your audience will be interested in.

## Step five:
## Boost your message!

Once you have your visuals, you need to make the best use of them during the presentation to reinforce what you're saying.

- ✓ Unless a slide or visual is completely obvious or self-explanatory, you need to discuss it – or at least refer to it. It's amazing how many presenters put up a visual and then don't even mention it!

- ✓ Make sure you don't block your audience's view; you could even step aside for a moment and let people look at it properly.

- ✓ Once the slide or visual has made its point, change it – otherwise it might become a distraction.

## TOP TIP

A visual doesn't always have to be on a slide: if you are presenting in-person, it can also be a prop – a 3D object that you pass round, for the audience to examine. If you're enthusing about your company's new design of reusable coffee cup, for example, there's nothing like letting people handle a real one for ensuring that they remember it.

## Common mistakes

✗   You over-complicate things

'Keep it simple' is the implicit message throughout all the guidelines above, but it's worth reiterating here. It's extraordinary how many people forget it. Sometimes this is due, ironically, to lack of time – it can take longer to think through a point and boil it down to its essentials than simply to slap down all the available material. It can also be easy to fall for lovely software and graphics packages that tempt you to create fancy effects and animations. Don't! If you bewilder your audience or distract people from your main message, all your efforts will be wasted.

✗   You forget to check for errors

This is one of the commonest ways to shoot yourself in the foot. Your presentation looks lovely, your arguments are sound, your visuals are punchy and effective, BUT . . . you misspell the chief executive's name or the title on the first slide. Zap goes your credibility and you'll have to work very hard to build it back up!

## BUSINESS ESSENTIALS

✔ Make sure everything looks consistent and professional, and fits with your business image or brand.

✔ Use big font sizes that can be read from the back row.

✔ Cut out all but essential text.

✔ Check that all fonts and colours are clear and readable.

✔ Follow a logical sequence throughout your presentation.

✔ Decide whether visuals are really necessary.

✔ If so, make sure they're well designed and appropriate to the rest of your presentation.

✔ Think about using props in addition to your visuals.

✔ Be careful not to get too complicated.

✔ Check for errors!

# 6
# Fighting back against nerves

Being overcome by nerves can be a completely debilitating experience that sabotages our ability to communicate well and to demonstrate how well we can do our job. If you're prone to feeling nervous, presentations are probably one of the most stressful situations you can be placed in.

The body's nervous reaction to speaking in public, whether it's making a presentation to customers or colleagues, or even making an intervention during an internal meeting can, if left unchecked, rob us in just a few seconds of the confidence and experience built up during the course of our career.

If you do suffer from nerves in some work situations, take comfort in knowing that you're not alone and that with the help of a few simple techniques, you can kick nerves into touch. It's always tempting to think that a problem will just go away, but tackling nerves will offer a range of positive results, including being able to be yourself, contributing to events in the way you know you can deep down and getting the amazing next job you deserve. Overcoming nerves is a great first step on the journey to full confidence.

## Step one:
## Start off with some positive thinking

It's always hard to be objective when you're very worried about something, but it really is the first step on the road to taking charge of yourself. If you see yourself failing at something in your mind's eye, you're much more likely to end up with a disaster on your hands. Try to get your imagination under control and instead of seeing yourself getting it all spectacularly wrong, see yourself succeeding brilliantly. Your body will follow the cues from your mind, so train your mind to be positive and to 'invite' success for yourself.

### TOP TIP

Don't let negative images or words creep in and get in the way of your preparation; if you feel your positive attitude starting to slip, take a short break and start again.

## Step two:
## Breathe!

When people get nervous, they panic and speak before they've thought things through. If you're worried that your mouth may run away with you, manage your breathing. Most people aren't particularly good at doing this, but it's the key to giving yourself space to observe and hear what's going on. This is an important technique to learn if you have to participate in meetings or if people will be asking you questions as part of your presentation – being sensitive to the needs of others and different situations is an important part of being able to say the right thing at the right time.

> **TOP TIP**
>
> If you're in an important meeting that you want to contribute to, give yourself time to take in the information you need and formulate what you're going to say. Don't rush in, but breathe calmly and don't worry about short silences.

## Step three:
## Don't let shyness be a barrier

If you're naturally a shy person then public speaking can seem a huge barrier to overcome. Strangely, though, some of the best presenters are introverts and many have severe bouts of nerves before taking the stage and delivering a polished performance.

One good way of lessening the fear of public speaking is to think of it as having a conversation, rather than giving a talk. It also helps to break the ice by talking to a few people from your audience first; this will help you make a connection with them that you can use and build on while you're in front of them. This works just as well online as in-person. Be friendly, smile, look people in the eyes, ask questions if appropriate, and take the listening time to breathe, relax and enjoy the experience if you can.

## Step four:
## Understand the physical effects of worry

Although the effects of a bout of nerves show themselves physically, it's actually our state of mind that triggers them. Fears that we'll make a fool of ourselves or that we won't achieve our aims commonly drive our nervous reactions, which are often known as the 'fight or flight' response.

Thousands of years ago, when we were surviving in a physically hostile world that was populated by human predators or enemies, our fight or flight response enabled us to fuel our strength and overpower a beast or build our speed and outrun something that was threatening us. In the moment of need, adrenalin would be released, our hearts would pump faster, our blood would be super-oxygenated and our muscles would be fed to achieve higher levels of performance. This is what enabled human beings to survive and build the (relatively) safe, sophisticated and cerebral world that we enjoy today. However, in spite of our successful emergence from the primitive world, our bodies still react to fear – whether it be real or imagined – in the same way.

When we're giving a presentation, our fear of failure gives rise to the fight or flight response along with its characteristic bodily reactions, but these now have nowhere to go. We don't take flight and neither do we fight, but instead stand still, tell ourselves not to be so silly and try to combat the panic. By this stage, there's no point in trying to use our mind to control the effects of fear as our body has taken control. The fact that we can't do anything about it gives rise to further feelings of anxiety and sends a message to the body to try harder because the threat has not disappeared and there's still work to be done. More adrenalin . . . faster heartbeat . . . busy muscles . . . and so it goes on. Trying to break this cycle is the challenge of overcoming nerves and it can be tackled in two ways; through the mind and through the body.

## 1 *Overcome nerves through the mind*

✓ Use visualization as a technique for removing fear. Imagine your audience receiving your information enthusiastically, being interested in what you're saying, and applauding or sending messages of thanks in the chat when you've finished. Enhance this image with feelings of satisfaction, achievement and pride. Watch yourself feeling confident and happy and acknowledging people who talk to you afterwards and congratulate you on your performance.

✓ Think through your presentation or performance beforehand so that you're both practically and mentally prepared. If you're likely to be asked questions on your presentation, imagine what these might be and prepare some answers. If it helps, write them down, read over them a few times and tick them off your 'checklist' of things to prepare.

✓ Get as much information as possible. This will help you target your talk appropriately and demonstrate that you understand your audience's perspective and needs well. Being able to show that you've taken the time to do this will help win them over and get them on your side.

Working through the exercises above will help remove any perceived threats and will fill your mind with positive images. Cancelling out the threat in any given situation means that you're a lot less likely to have an adverse physical response to it.

## 2 *Overcome nerves through the body*

Some of these well-known relaxation techniques will help prevent your body from triggering the 'fear response'.

✓ Spend a few minutes to calm your breathing and to take attention away from the impending perform-ance. Breathe deeply into your stomach, hold your breath for a few seconds, then breathe out again. Do this several times in a quiet spot away from the venue or your computer.

✓ Relax your body. Sit in a chair and concentrate on each muscle group one by one. Working from your feet to your forehead, contract and then relax your muscles. Feel the difference. If you find yourself becoming tense again, go back to the problem area and try again, breathing deeply and steadily as you do so.

✓ Have some water before your performance to prevent you from drying up and keep another glass beside you so that you can refresh your mouth as you go.

**TOP TIP**

Overcoming nerves is hard work, but it's well worth spending the time to do it. Succeeding means that you'll be able to express yourself well and with confidence in any situation. This will help you in all areas of your life.

### Common mistakes

✗ You put yourself under too much pressure

It's completely counter-productive to beat yourself up about getting nervous. What is the point? The best thing to do is to set yourself reasonable goals, take things one step at a time and give yourself an opportunity to celebrate each small success and build upon it incrementally. If you challenge yourself by putting yourself in extreme situations, you run the risk of failing in those extremes and it can be very difficult to recover from that. Be gentle with yourself and try to build your confidence steadily and soundly.

✗ You pretend you don't suffer from nerves

When people want to appear confident and competent, they often won't own up to suffering from nerves and end up playing a part, rather than being themselves. This is a common mistake, which at best makes it seem as if you're suppressing the real 'you', but at worst, can make you seem arrogant. Putting on a front can be helpful in some situations, for example, if the real you is hidden somewhere in the role that you've decided to act out, but removing who you are by 'being someone else' isn't a good way to overcome nerves. Hiding yourself away won't help and in fact sometimes it's just better to acknowledge your perceived shortcomings and turn to someone who can help you find an appropriate way through.

✗ You think the problem will go away

Many would-be presenters who are overcome by nerves avoid dealing with them, thinking that they just have to get through their ordeal and somehow arrive at the other side. This is perfectly true, but it can be life-enhancing to face your fears and find a dignified way through. Often, when we look our fears in the face, they begin to subside, especially if we practise techniques to master them. Rehearsing is extremely helpful, whether it's in front of friends, family or even just in front of the mirror. If you're able to video yourself rehearsing, so much the better; you'll learn a lot.

## BUSINESS ESSENTIALS

✔ Think positive!

✔ Breathe!

✔ Build a connection with your audience to dispel shyness.

✔ Learn how to use relaxation techniques.

# 7
# Boosting your 'live' message with your body language

We all know that real communication is not just a matter of making a noise. But did you realize just how little impact what we actually say has on people we're speaking to? In a live situation, like a presentation, between 55 and 65 per cent of your meaning is communicated by your body language – your posture, movements and facial expressions – and 38 per cent comes from your tone of voice. That leaves just 7 per cent to be conveyed by the words you use!

In addition, researchers also agree that the verbal part of the communication is used to convey information, while the non-verbal part is used to convey values, feelings and attitudes – the things that build rapport.

It's obvious, then, that if you can learn to understand and control body language in a conscious way, you can make an enormous difference to the impact you have on your audience. This chapter will help you to use the different forms of non-verbal communication to help get your message across effectively and to build rapport with your listeners.

## Step one:
## Make a good entrance

People, like animals, are territorial and instinctively perceive new spaces – like an unfamiliar presentation room – as hostile territory. As a result, it's natural, if you have not been in the room before, to decrease your speed as you enter it, and this can make you look as if you lack confidence.

There are a number of things you can do about this:

- be in the room first, before your audience arrives, so that you already 'own' the space; this applies to virtual spaces as well as real ones;

- if in-person, familiarize yourself with the room before the presentation, so that when you do enter you are more relaxed and in charge;

- arrive early in live and virtual situations, so that you are comfortable with the tech set-up, the height of your chair, how you look on screen;

- if in-person, make a point of going into the room at an even speed or even stopping at the door before entering.

## Step two:
## Use positive postures

One of the biggest giveaway indications of nerves is your posture. And interestingly enough if you look nervous, rather than getting people's sympathy, you tend to make your audience inclined to feel hostile towards you. Self-defence teachers know this: they teach their pupils to carry themselves in a self-confident and upright manner, as people who walk in a timid or frightened way are much more likely to be victims of attack.

To make sure that your posture doesn't betray your nerves as you speak:

- stand or sit up straight with your feet slightly apart; keep your head up and think generally about taking up as much space as you can. It might help to keep in mind the saying, 'think tall and you'll be tall' – this will automatically help you to adopt a much more confident posture;

- don't hold your arms in front of your body too much. People feeling nervous or unsure of themselves will often 'protect' themselves. Nothing can make you look more uncomfortable or nervous than appearing in front of a presentation audience with your arms crossed or holding something!

## TOP TIP

If you can avoid it, don't have any piece of furniture or other object between you and your audience/ screen – it can act as a barrier and create a distance between you. However, if you find you have a tendency to shuffle your feet nervously in-person, you could try positioning a table behind you so that you can lean back on the edge of it.

## Step three:
## Be natural with gestures

It's easy to worry too much about gestures. With a few exceptions, most gestures are fine – provided that they feel natural to you. After all, for most people, gestures are an extension of their personality and it can make you feel uncomfortable and unnatural if you try to repress them.

Having said this, there are a few useful things to remember about gestures:

- never make a rude one (obviously!);

- try not to make the same gesture too many times, or it will turn into a mannerism that could distract your audience; they might find it tempting to count how many times you wag your forefinger, rather than listening to what you're saying;

- be on the lookout for distracting habits you acquire only when you're under stress, such as foot-shuffling or lip-licking. If you know what these are, you might be able to eliminate them, or at least minimize them;

- if you find it difficult to know what to do with your hands, you could try using a 'prop'. Many people use props to reinforce their messages, the most common being extensions of the hand such as a pen or pointer. Using a prop extends the space taken up by your body – and hence your territory – and you are perceived as more confident and powerful.

**TOP TIP**

No matter how nervous you are, try to avoid hand-to-face gestures such as touching your nose or rubbing your eye. These often mean you're not entirely comfortable with your subject matter and can signify that you're not being completely honest about something. Even if your listeners don't know this consciously, they will pick up on your discomfort.

## Step four:
## Keep up eye contact

It's true of all human interactions to say that the more eye contact we have with someone, the closer we tend to feel to them – and they to us. Often, we will avoid eye contact with someone we don't like, and if we do make it, we will adopt an unemotional stare, rather than a friendly gaze.

✔ When you're giving a presentation, keep your eye contact with people as normal as possible. Look at everyone in the room and on the screen, not just the person in the middle or at the front who you feel is on your side. That way, each member of your audience will begin to feel that they have forged some sort of personal bond with you and will be more receptive to your message.

**TOP TIP**

There are two useful things to remember about eye contact. First, lowered eyes make you look shy. Second, people will naturally follow your gaze and if you keep looking at the ceiling, so will they.

## Step five:
## Keep an eye on your timing

In normal conversation, another element that conveys information (often unconsciously) is the speed at which you talk. Speaking slowly can sometimes indicate that you're uncertain of what you're saying; speaking quickly may show that you're anxious or excited. These rules still apply to some degree when you're delivering a presentation, which may make you feel as if you're stuck between a rock and a hard place. As ever, though, going for the middle ground is much the safest option. Whether online or in-person, make sure you have a clock, watch or mobile phone visible, so that you can keep an eye on the time.

✓ Although it's important to speak slowly enough to enable your audience to hear what you're saying, don't overdo it or you'll sound hesitant. Conversely, you also need to guard against gabbling – it's a natural tendency to speak faster than usual if you're nervous and if you're normally a fast talker anyway, you can completely lose your audience!

## Step six:
## Watch your tone and mannerisms

The manner in which you speak during your presentation is almost more important than anything else. If you think about it, even a simple word like 'hello' can have multiple different meanings – friendly, hostile, surprised, suspicious, offhand and many others – depending on how you say it, so you need to be careful about what tone of voice you use. There are a number of things to think about here.

✓ Try to sound friendly, but not so casual that you lose your authority.

✓ At the same time, don't be too bossy – this is a presentation, not a lecture.

✓ It's better to be too loud than too soft; nothing is more trying for an audience than a mumbling presenter.

✓ Ask someone you trust to listen to you and check that you are not swallowing words (easy to do when you're nervous) – in other words, that the ends of your sentences don't die away and become inaudible. To a listener, this makes it seem as if the presentation is repeatedly grinding to a halt.

✓ Bear in mind that too many 'ums', 'ers' and hesitations make you sound unprofessional and can be irritating to listen to. Plenty of rehearsal should solve this issue.

### TOP TIP

As with physical gestures, most catchphrases – 'as I say', 'basically', 'you know', for example – are fine unless they're used too frequently, when they become a distracting mannerism. Again, when you practise, ask someone to keep an ear out for things like this. You may be so used to saying them that you don't notice you're doing it!

### Step seven:
### Remember your facial expressions

As with eye contact, people's emotions towards us are influenced by our facial expressions. In fact, this is so much the case that if someone continually shows the 'wrong' facial expressions, or doesn't change their expression at all, we find it hard to warm to them.

While this doesn't mean you should grin manically at your audience throughout your presentation, it does mean that you don't have to be too guarded in your expressions – and it won't ruin your image or make you appear unprofessional if you smile occasionally. In fact, smiling will help put you and your audience at ease. It's not appropriate at all times, of course – if you're delivering bad news of some type, for example – but in the normal run of things, it does no harm.

### Step eight:
### Match your clothes to the occasion

According to the experts, people form 90 per cent of their opinion about someone within the first 90 seconds of meeting them, which means that your audience will be making judgements about you long before you even open your mouth.

What you wear is therefore your first means of communicating something about yourself, and will help your audience to relate to you . . . or not. As a rough rule of thumb, people tend to like people who are like them – so it's best to dress in the same sort of way as those you'll be presenting to. If you're presenting informally to a group of colleagues, for example, you can wear normal office attire, while a more formal suit might be better for a meeting of government bureaucrats.

If in doubt, it's probably best to err on the side of restraint. That way, the worst you can do is to present a blank canvas that doesn't distract your audience from what you have to say. After all, you want your message to be the point of focus in your presentation, not your personality.

## Common mistakes

✗ You lack 'congruence'

Because body language is something that occurs naturally, whether or not we are conscious of it, it's impossible to control every last aspect of it. This means that if you are talking about something you don't really believe in, or if you're not entirely comfortable with what you are saying, your body language will subtly 'leak' this somewhere along the line. This lack of 'congruence' between your words and your body language will be picked up on by your audience and they are likely to feel suspicious and distrustful of you and your message. The only answer is to be authentic in what you say and your body language will reinforce that message naturally.

✗ You over-do things

When you become conscious of all the ways in which you communicate non-verbally with others, it can suddenly become terribly easy to over-do them . . . your eye contact is a little too intense, your posture a little too confident, your gestures a little too controlled and so on. And, just as is the case with a lack of congruence, this can make you come across as insincere and inauthentic and may turn your audience against you. To be effective, body language must be subtle and seem completely natural – and the only way to achieve this is to practise over and over again. Try watching yourself in a mirror as you rehearse your presentation or ask someone you trust to observe you and give you honest feedback. Eventually, if you practise enough, controlling your body language will become second nature to you.

## BUSINESS ESSENTIALS

✓ Make a positive entrance so that you, and not your audience, 'own' the space.

✓ Adopt a confident posture that will reduce any inclination in people to be hostile towards you.

✓ Be natural in your gestures, while taking care that no individual gesture becomes a mannerism through being used too frequently.

✓ Maintain regular eye contact with all members of your audience to build rapport.

✓ Speak at the right speed – not so slowly that you sound hesitant, but not so fast that you gabble.

✓ Check that your tone of voice makes your message friendly and accessible, while still retaining its authority.

✓ Don't worry about being too guarded in your facial expressions or you may come across as odd.

✓ Dress to flatter your audience – in other words, in a similar way to them.

# 8
# Surviving worst-case scenarios

In an ideal world, everything would always go as planned. Sadly, the world is anything but ideal and as a result, hardly anything ever does! This can be pretty disconcerting, particularly if you're in a situation where you're 'on show', such as giving a presentation. However, there are very few circumstances that are completely irredeemable, unless you panic.

It's well worth spending some time thinking through all the things that could possibly go wrong and (if possible) taking preventive action, or (if not) planning what to do in the event. Obviously an in-person presentation at a venue raises more issues than an online one from home so let's start with that.

## In-person presentations

### Step one:
### Make sure you can handle the technology and equipment you need

Technology is a potential problem for every presenter. Even the best-designed presentation will fail if the technology you use to deliver it goes wrong, so it's really important to check everything beforehand.

### *Technology*

✓ Unless you're using your own equipment, make sure that your presentation will work on what's provided.

✓ Have you checked that your presentation uploads and runs as expected on the computer? For example, does this machine run the same software version that you use? You may be able to run newer presentations under older versions of PowerPoint, for example, but extra features (such as animations or links to other applications) may not work. Check that they do.

✓ Are you connected to the right wi-fi network if required?

✓ Are there enough power points, of the right kinds and in the right places? Will you need extension cables or extra plug sockets, or do you need to rearrange the room?

✓ Do the connections between different pieces of equipment – from the handheld 'clicker' to the laptop, for example – work properly? Sometimes you may need particular cables e.g. for connecting a laptop to a projector; make sure you have them before you set up.

✓ If at all possible, run your presentation through from beginning to end in situ.

### *Other equipment*

✓ Make sure you have spares of everything you could need – your notes printed out, in case the tech goes, extra handouts if you are using them, whiteboard pens, laptop power cable, mobile phone battery and so on.

✓ If you are using index prompt cards, make sure that they are numbered so that you can easily find your place if they get muddled or you drop them.

✓ Check that any lectern or stand is at the right height for you.

✓ Confirm that people will be able to hear properly from all parts of the room, particularly if you're using sound effects or a microphone.

✓ Familiarize yourself with how to operate all the lights, air-conditioning, heating and so on.

✓ Make sure you know where all the amenities are – coffee rooms, toilets, reception areas, phones, for example – not just for your own information, but so that you can answer if asked by an audience member.

### TOP TIP

Be prepared! If you're presenting at your own office, do a practice run-through the day or a few hours before your presentation, so you can check everything mentioned above. If you're presenting elsewhere, liaise with your contact at the venue to find out as much as you can about what equipment is available and what you'll be expected to bring. Arrive at the venue in plenty of time so that you can practise there, too.

**Step two:**
**Manage the audience**

*Arrange the seating sensibly*

There's nothing worse, when presenting, than facing an audience that is scattered all over the room or, even worse, huddled into the back rows of seats leaving a great gulf between you and them. Even the greatest speaker will have difficulty building energy or creating rapport in such circumstances. There are a couple of ways you can prevent such a situation arising.

- If at all possible, find out how many people are coming and put out just enough seats, plus a couple of extras; arrange them in an arc facing you.

- If you have no idea of, or control over, the numbers attending, tape off the back row of seats and put a 'Reserved' sign on them; once the front rows are full, remove the sign and let the last arrivals sit at the back.

### Think about the staging

There are a few other tips for staging the presentation that will also help things run smoothly and enable you to engage with your audience.

- Make sure you're not standing with your back to a window or else you'll appear as a silhouette to your listeners.

- Check that you have somewhere – such as a table or chair – to put your notes, handouts, bag, coat and anything else you have with you.

- If you need to darken the room, make sure you know where light switches are and how curtains or blinds close.

- Try sitting in different parts of the room to check that all members of the audience will be able to see properly.

✓ If possible, make sure there's nothing – like a desk or table – between you and your audience. Psychologically, it will act as a barrier and you will have to work that much harder to create rapport.

### TOP TIP

Audiences have a very short attention span – most adults cannot concentrate for more than seven to 10 minutes. To prevent people from wriggling, chatting or switching off, it's a good idea to break your presentation into easily digestible sections and change the pace or create a diversion at regular intervals.

BUSINESS ESSENTIALS

### Step three:
### Deal with disruptions

Interruptions can put you off your stride, so take preventative action before your presentation begins.

✓ Make sure the room is booked well in advance – you don't want another group of people arriving at the same time expecting to have a meeting there!

✓ Ask everyone attending to switch off their phone and make sure you switch your own off, if not using it for the presentation.

✓ Put a sign on the door to stop people from barging in unintentionally.

✓ Check that there's no regular interruption planned, such as a fire drill. If there is, plan a break around it, or at least tell the audience what will be happening beforehand.

✓ Fill the seats from the front, as described earlier; this has the added benefit of preventing late arrivals from walking all the way to the front and climbing across other people to find somewhere to sit.

✓ If the presentation is likely to be a long one, make sure you schedule plenty of breaks – preferably on the hour, every hour. This helps to eliminate surreptitious escapes to the toilet and maintains people's concentration.

**TOP TIP**

You can never expect to eliminate all kinds of interruption, so the golden rule, if you are interrupted, is to acknowledge it rather than trying to carry on regardless. If you pause and laugh while a jet plane thunders overhead, for example, the audience will probably laugh too, and the whole episode will actually work to your advantage by creating a bond between you.

### Step four:
### Survive unexpected time issues

Uncertainty about or problems with the time available can throw a presenter completely. Say, for example, the meeting before yours overruns and cuts your time severely ... what do you do then? The two scenarios below cover most contingencies.

## 1 *You find you have 20 minutes instead of the hour you planned on*

Talking quickly isn't the answer! Decide swiftly what proportion of the 20 minutes each part of your presentation should take. Is there any section that could be omitted altogether? Then keep your eye on your watch as you speak and limit yourself to the key concept in each portion.

## 2 *A vital member of the audience has to leave before you've reached your key points*

Say the finance director, who has ultimate say over whether his company buys your products, tells you he has to leave early. This could be disastrous. However, there's an old rule regarding presentations: tell people what you're going to tell them, tell them, and then tell them what you told them. If you follow this rule when creating your presentation in the first place, you won't be caught out this way.

✔ Always mention your main point and major supporting points within the first few minutes of any presentation.

✔ If you're using slides, always have one that contains the main point and the key points.

If, however, you've made the fatal error of trying to save the best for last, ask the decision-maker for a moment to summarize (anyone will give you a moment if you ask nicely). Then state, in one sentence, the single point you want the decision-maker to remember and, if you have a chance, the two concepts that best support that point.

## TOP TIP

It's always worth considering contingencies when you're creating a presentation. What would you leave out if your time were halved? What would your key messages be if you had five minutes to tell someone about them?

## Step five:
## Answer difficult questions

Some presenters dread questions from the audience more than anything else, as it's impossible to know what might come up or whether someone might have a particular agenda attached to the question they ask. However, most tricky questions tend to fall into one of only a few categories, and if you recognize these, it will help you know how to answer.

| Type of question | Best response |
|---|---|
| The concealed objection – e.g. 'How come the price is so high?' | Don't get defensive.<br>Ask them to clarify – e.g. 'What makes you feel that the price is too high?'<br>Put it in perspective – e.g. 'It's only a few pence more expensive than its nearest rival.'<br>Give the compensating benefits – '… and the quality is much higher, so it's actually better value for money.' |
| The display question, often intended to demonstrate the questioner's own expertise | Play along and don't be afraid to acknowledge how clever they are publicly. 'Of course, you're right – I didn't mention it, simply because I thought it might be too technical for this occasion.' |
| The challenge question, which usually means you've trespassed on someone's area of knowledge | Back down, concede all territorial rights and perhaps consult their opinion. 'I'm sorry, I meant the transport policy in the West Midlands, not in the whole of the UK – which of course you know more about than I do. Would you say it's the same across the board?' |

| The defensive question, which tends to mean something you've proposed is a threat to the questioner – e.g. 'Do you really think it's a good idea to let managers train their own staff?' | Try to question the questioner. 'Could you explain your concerns further, perhaps?' Throw the question open to the floor … do other people feel managers aren't qualified to train their staff? If it's not within your remit, refer the questioner to someone who can provide answers. |
|---|---|
| The question you plan to discuss in detail later | Provide a brief answer, then say that you plan to cover the subject properly later. Don't ask the questioner to wait until you reach the point at which you originally intended to discuss the subject or everyone will focus on the unanswered question instead of listening to you. In a meeting setting or small presentation, don't ask people to keep their questions for the end as this suggests that you're not confident enough to deal with interruptions. |

### TOP TIP

If nothing else, making sure that you know your stuff and keep calm will usually be enough to deal with most questions that you might face.

### Step six:
### Don't let nerves get to you

Almost everyone, even those with lots of experience, suffers from nerves to some degree when they have to present to a group of people. And nerves can make you prone to accidents and stumbling.

However, the one key to solving almost all of these is understanding what causes an attack of nerves: fear, usually of what could possibly go wrong. This is why you generally feel better once you've got going: your equipment's working OK, the audience hasn't switched off and gone to sleep, you haven't made an idiot of yourself and so on.

The more you pre-empt your fear, then, by doing your preparation thoroughly and taking preventive measures against things that could go wrong, the less nervous you will feel and the less likely you'll be to come a cropper. However, even with all the preparation in the world, things can still sometimes go awry. If they do, don't panic – you can still win through. Here are some of the most common nerve-induced pitfalls and what to do about them:

### *You lose your train of thought mid-sentence*

Smile, say 'excuse me' or 'I'm sorry' and start again. Try not to panic or get flustered: it's not the end of the world and everyone has lost track of an idea at least once in their lives. People want you to succeed and are generally sympathetic. Keep smiling.

### *Your throat dries up*

Actors have a good trick for dealing with this. Roll a tiny piece of paper into a small ball and place it between your gum and the inside of your cheek at the back of your mouth. It will stimulate the flow of saliva, just like that little roll of cotton wool the dentist uses. Try this in private first, however, so you are sure you are comfortable.

### *You drop your notes on the floor*

Make a joke about your clumsiness, pick them up and take a few moments to put them in order. (Now is the time to be grateful you have numbered them.)

## Online presentations

### Hacking

Online presentations can be subject to this, via 'room' break-ins. Several things can help prevent it.

✓ Always set up meetings using the 'waiting room' option on your video-conferencing software and don't allow participants to arrive without being 'allowed in' by you. This is relatively easy with small groups and in your own company, but not so simple if you are presenting to clients and suppliers. If possible, try to get the names of all the attendees before the presentation so that you can manage who attends. Or ask someone from the client company to manage the arrivals for you, since they are more likely to know staff names.

✓ Ask participants not to share the presentation/ meeting link with anyone else and especially not on social media.

### Interruptions

If you are presenting online at work, you will hopefully be able to manage interruptions by closing your office door, diverting your landline and switching mobile phones to silent. However, at home this is harder. The following are worth trying.

✓ Work in a room with a door, and put a note on the door to remind other people in your household not to come in.

✓ Put pets in another room and close the door. Better still, put the cat out and get someone else to walk the dog!

✓ If you have small children, ask another adult or older child to keep them out of the room.

✓ Unplug your doorbell!

✓ If you are interrupted, try not to get flustered, pause the presentation and deal with it. Remember that your audience will have all experienced the same issues and making light of it will endear you to them and make the occasion more memorable.

### *Muting*

Set up your meeting to mute participants on entry, and ask everyone to mute both their phones and any notifications that might come through on the device they are using to watch the presentation. Pinging email notifications can be distracting. Be sure to switch yours off, too. Depending on the type of presentation, you can either unmute participants as required or ask them to do it themselves.

### *Broadband issues*

Hopefully, your work broadband is fast enough to cope with any type of online activity, but at home this is not always the case. So, before your presentation, give the following a go.

✓ Can you move your computer closer to the router? The closer you are, the better the broadband speed and quality.

- Make sure other members of your household are not streaming videos or gaming across a network at the same time as your presentation; again, this will reduce broadband speed and quality.

- If the broadband speed and quality are not great in any room in your home, a wi-fi extender might improve it. If you work from home for a company, they should provide this.

If your broadband does crash during your presentation, try not to panic and simply reboot it. If this doesn't work, you will have to reschedule. Again, your audience will have experienced similar issues in their own working lives and will, hopefully, be understanding!

## Common mistakes

✗ You don't rehearse

Almost every piece of advice in this action list points to one thing: you MUST PRACTISE! With plenty of rehearsal, your confidence will be sufficient to see you through just about any disaster. It's not enough to say your presentation over to yourself in your head, as it's very different when you have to get up and do it in front of an audience. Choose a friend or colleague whom you trust and ask them if they will watch you and give you honest feedback. As an absolute minimum, stand in front of a mirror and run through the presentation, checking yourself as critically as you can.

## BUSINESS ESSENTIALS

✓ In order to pre-empt disasters with equipment, check thoroughly that everything works before the presentation starts.

✓ Arrange the seating and staging in the best way to help build rapport with your audience and to maintain their concentration.

✓ Take pre-emptive measures to avoid interruptions.

✓ Have contingency plans in case the time available alters significantly.

✓ Learn to handle difficult questions.

✓ Manage your nerves by addressing the fear behind them.

✓ Practise, practise, practise.

# Where to find more help

The Internet is full of video guides to presenting; here are two of the best places to start.

Ted Talks
The global online learning network has tons of advice and examples of how to give a good presentation. Here's a good place to start: ted.com/playlists/574/how_to_make_a_great_presentation

Toastmasters
An international organization devoted to the art of public speaking and communication. Lots of free resources available on their website. toastmasters.org/resources/public-speaking-tips

*Ted Talks: The Official TED Guide to Public Speaking*
Chris Anderson, Head of TED, Hodder and Stoughton, 2016

*Presentation Skills for Students*
Joan van Emden & Lucinda Becker, Palgrave, 2016

# Index